AUTUMN

in the Forest

A *Seasons in the Forest* book

Field Guides for Little Naturalists

For Bill, who teaches children and me
about the life of the forest.

Fly away,
fly away,
fly away, Goose.

There's a chill in the air.

The wind's on the loose.

Fade away,
fade away,
fade away, green.

Let scarlets blaze,

let yellows gleam.

Fall away,
    fall away,
        fall away, leaves.

Soften the ground,

make space in the trees.

Hide away,
hide away,
hide away, Squirrel.

Store winter's nuts

as maple seeds twirl.

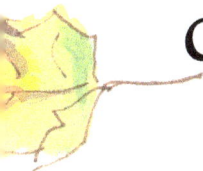

Scratch away,
scratch away,
scratch away, Bear.

Loosen the dirt
in last winter's lair.

The forest is changing.

Autumn is here.

Make preparations

as winter draws near.

White Oak

Shagbark Hickory

Eastern
White Pine

American Beech

In the fall, forest animals prepare for winter. Some fly away to warmer places, others stay. Fur changes to white on some animals. They eat a lot of food. Their fat will keep them warm during the long sleep of winter.

Plants prepare for winter, too. They make seeds that fall to the ground and get covered by leaves until spring. When the world warms, some seeds will sprout into new young plants.

Acorns are seeds. How many can you put in your pocket? What about pine cones? Pine cones hide tiny seeds inside. How many seeds can you find, little squirrel?

About the author:

Christine Copeland lives in the forest of Massachusetts with her husband Bill, a pediatrician, naturalist and teacher, and their dogs and cat. Her sons have fledged but return seasonally. She is grateful to be visited by many birds and other animals throughout the year. Christine has a BFA from Cornell University and a Masters in Education from Antioch New England. She is an author/illustrator and also paints in oil. Her work can be seen at christinecopelandbooks.com and bcc-studios.com/paintings.

www.ingramcontent.com/pod-product-compliance
Lightning Source LLC
Chambersburg PA
CBHW042334030426
42335CB00027B/3340